ASK AND IT WILL BE GIVEN TO YOU,
SEEK AND YOU WILL FIND,
KNOCK AND THE DOOR WILL BE OPENED TO YOU

⟫⟫⟩ THE ANNUNCIATION ⟨⟪⟪

The word *annunciation* has the same Latin root, and the same meaning as the word *announcement*.

God sent the angel Gabriel to Nazareth, a town in Galilee, to seek out Mary.

The angel appeared to her and said, "God is with you." Mary was surprised and concerned.

"Do not be afraid, Mary," said the angel. "God loves you. I am here to tell you that you will give birth to a son, and you will call him Jesus. He will be great and will be called the Son of God.

The Lord God will make him King, and his kingdom will never end."

"I will do as God says," Mary answered. "May your words to me come true."

THE ANNUNCIATION *by Leonardo da Vinci, created around 1472–1475*

In Leonardo's painting Mary is reading the Bible as the angel appears to her. The gesture of her left hand shows surprise. The angel holds a white lily, the symbol of a pure heart, in his left hand. His right hand is raised in a gesture of blessing. There are circles of light over the heads of Mary and Gabriel. Such a circle, or *halo*, is a symbol of holiness. In art, both Mary and Jesus are often shown wearing red and blue clothes. The color red was used as a symbol of loyalty and sacrifice. Blue was a symbol of a holy life, and also of royalty. Blue dye was rare. In ancient times blue paint was made from ground lapis lazuli, a semi-precious stone that was more expensive than gold.

Leonardo da Vinci is one of the greatest Italian artists of the era we call the *Renaissance* – which saw the flourishing of arts in Europe from the 14th through 16th centuries. Leonardo created this painting when he studied at the workshop of his teacher, Andrea del Verrocchio, in Florence. Some portions of the painting are thought to have been created by Verrocchio.

The Feast of the Annunciation is celebrated in spring. Western churches, such as the *Catholic church*, celebrate it on March 25. They use the *Gregorian* calendar, named after Pope Gregory XIII. Some Eastern churches such as the *Russian* and *Greek Orthodox churches*, use the *Julian* calendar, created by the order of Julius Caesar. They celebrate the Annunciation on April 7.

We see beautiful white and purple spring flowers in Leonardo's painting. We also see a springtime garden in the *Annunciation* painting by Beatrice Emma Parsons, a 19th-century English artist. The style and mood of her work is very different from that of Leonardo. That's not surprising: It was created more than 400 years after Leonardo's *Annunciation*. Beatrice Parson's painting looks much more realistic, almost like a photograph. We see some familiar symbols – white lilies are blooming in Mary's garden. There are also red roses, sprinkled around, like drops of blood. Remember, red is the symbol of sacrifice. The angel doesn't seem to have wings, and instead of a halo there is a touch of sunset light around his head.

THE ANNUNCIATION *by Beatrice Emma Parsons, created around 1897-1899*

NATIVITY *by Gerard David, 1510–1515*

The word *nativity* has the same Latin root as the word *native*. *Nativity* means *birth*.

Mary, the mother of Jesus, and his stepfather, Joseph, lived in Israel. At that time Israel was a part of the Roman Empire. Roman Emperor Caesar Augustus ordered that a *census* should be taken of the entire Roman world. A *census* is writing down the names of all the people in the land and counting everyone.

To be counted in the census, Mary and Joseph came to the town of Bethlehem. But so many people came there at the same time, that there was no place to stay. The only room they could find was a barn at one of the town inns. And that's where baby Jesus was born. Mary and Joseph did not have a bed for him, so Mary laid him in a manger. A *manger* is a place where they put grass and straw to feed cows, goats, sheep, and other animals. Churches celebrate the Feast of the Nativity on December 25 (or January 7, Julian calendar).

Gerard David lived and worked in the Renaissance era, like Leonardo da Vinci. But while Leonardo lived in Italy, Gerard David was from the Netherlands. In Gerard David's painting Mary and Joseph look serious and almost sad, as if they know that Jesus would not be with them for long. The colors of their clothes and walls are dark. Next to the manger is a bread basket. It's a hint at the words of Jesus, "I am the bread which came down from Heaven."

In the *Nativity* painting by the 19th-century English painter Arthur Hughes, Mary is wrapping Jesus in a piece of cloth, while an angel holds the baby, and the other angel holds a lantern.

NATIVITY *by Arthur Hughes*
created around 1857–1858

ADORATION OF THE SHEPHERDS *by Hugo van der Goes, 1476-1478*

ADORATION OF THE SHEPHERDS

In the fields near Bethlehem there were shepherds keeping watch over their flocks at night. Suddenly, an angel appeared to them in a ray of light. They were scared, but the angel said, "Do not be afraid. I bring you good news that will cause great joy for all the people. Today in Bethlehem a Savior has been born to you. Go and look for him. You will find a baby lying in a manger."

The shepherds went to Bethlehem, found Mary, Joseph, and the baby, and spread the word that the baby was the new King of Israel and the Savior. In great joy, they praised God. But Mary was quiet. The Gospel of Luke says that she "treasured up all these things and thought about them in her heart." In Hugo van der Goes' painting *Adoration of the Shepherds* Mary is deep in thought.

THE THREE KINGS

When Jesus was born, a star appeared over Bethlehem. The star was seen by wise men far away in the East. These wise men are also known as *the Three Kings*, or the *Magi*, from the Latin word *magus – a wizard.* The Magi traveled to Jerusalem, the capital of the kingdom of Judea in the land of Israel. "Where is the new King?" they asked. "We saw his star when it rose and have come to greet him." At that time Judea was ruled by King Herod. Herod was an evil and cruel ruler. He was angry that the Magi called some newborn baby "the King of Israel." So he called the Magi secretly and found out from them the exact time the star had appeared. He sent them to Bethlehem and said, "Go and search carefully for the child. As soon as you find him, let me know, so that I too may go and bow to him." The Magi went on their way, and the star led them all the way to Bethlehem. When they saw Jesus and Mary, they bowed down, opened their treasure chests, and gave the baby the gifts they brought with them – gold, frankincense, and myrrh. Frankincense and myrrh were made from the sap of rare trees and used in medicine and in making perfumes. That night an angel appeared to the Magi in a dream and warned them not to go back to Jerusalem, nor tell King Herod where Jesus was. So the Magi returned to their country by a different road.

THE ADORATION OF THE MAGI *by Gentile da Fabriano, 1423*

THE STAR OF BETHLEHEM *by Edward Burne-Jones, 1890*

Separated by over 450 years, the two paintings on these pages tell the story of the Magi in amazing color and detail. The three kings take off their crowns as they bow to Jesus. Silent, they hold boxes and jars with their precious gifts. Their faces are serious.

Italian artist Gentile da Fabriano painted in the ***Gothic*** style that had developed in Europe in the ***Middle Ages***, before the Renaissance took root in Italy. He used a lot of gold, decoration, and rich detail. Take a look at the designs of the Magi's clothes and crowns!

Working at the end of the 19th century, English artist Edward Burne-Jones was part of the ***Pre-Raphaelite*** art movement. ***Raphael*** was one of the greatest artists of the Italian Renaissance. But Pre-Raphaelite artists tried to bring back the art of the Middle Ages that came before the Renaissance (***pre-*** means ***before***). That's why you can see some elements of the Gothic style in Burne-Jones' painting. Like Gentile da Fabriano, he pays a lot of attention to the design of the Magi's clothes and crowns, and paints flowers, leaves, and grass with a lot of tiny detail. In his painting red roses bloom all around Mary and Jesus. Remember the meaning of this symbol? While in Fabriano's painting the star of Bethlehem is a burst of gold over Mary and Joseph, Burne-Jones shows it in the hands of an angel.

THE ESCAPE TO EGYPT

When the Magi left, an angel appeared to Joseph in a dream.

"Get up," he said, "take the child and his mother and escape to Egypt. Stay there until I tell you, because Herod is going to search for the child to kill him."

So Joseph and Mary left Bethlehem in the middle of the night, and traveled across the desert to Egypt.

When Herod realized that he had been outwitted by the Magi, he was furious, and he gave orders to kill all the boys younger than two years old in and around Bethlehem. Many kids died. Mary, Joseph, and Jesus stayed in Egypt until the death of King Herod.

MASSACRE OF THE INNOCENTS *by Léon Cogniet, 1824*

FLIGHT INTO EGYPT *by Eugène Girardet*

The two paintings on this page were created by two 19th-century French artists. Their style is very realistic. Hiding from King Herod's soldiers, a mother covers her baby's mouth to keep him quiet. The expression of fear on her face tells the story of the tragedy in Bethlehem. *The Flight into Egypt* shows Egyptian pyramids at sunrise. Eugène Girardet traveled to the Arab lands and painted scenes from everyday life in Algerian and Egyptian villages. Paintings portraying life in the Middle East and North Africa became known as *Orientalist Art*, from the Latin word *oriens* – the East.

CHRIST IN THE HOUSE OF HIS PARENTS *by John Everett Millais, 1849*

THE CHILDHOOD OF JESUS

We don't know much about Jesus' childhood. This painting by John Everett Millais is an attempt
to imagine his life in the house of his parents, Mary and Joseph. Millais belonged to the Pre-Raphaelite
art movement, and this painting has many features of the Pre-Raphaelite style. It is filled with bright
daylight, and portrays the scene and the emotions of its characters with realism and a lot of detail.

Joseph was a carpenter. In Millais' painting we see Jesus in Joseph's workshop. Joseph is working on
a wooden door. He has a couple helpers, including Anne, Jesus' grandmother. Jesus has cut his hand on
a nail. He shows Mary the wound on the palm of his hand. It looks like the wounds he will have dying
on the cross many years later. Mary offers her cheek for a kiss, her face sad and concerned. A little
boy brings some water to wash the wound. That's John the Baptist, who was a childhood friend of
Jesus. The water in a wooden bowl in his hands is a symbol of baptism. There are other symbols in
this painting: A dove sitting on the ladder by the wall is a symbol of the Holy Spirit, and, of course,
there is a red rose blooming outside.

THE FINDING OF THE SAVIOUR IN THE TEMPLE *by William Holman Hunt, 1860*

JESUS AT THE JERUSALEM TEMPLE

Every year Jesus' parents went to Jerusalem for the Festival of the Passover. When Jesus was 12, Mary and Joseph were traveling home from Jerusalem with a large group of relatives and friends, when they realized that Jesus was missing. They rushed back to Jerusalem, looking for him. Finally they found him in the court of the great Jerusalem Temple, sitting there among the teachers of the Jewish faith, listening to them and asking them questions. Everyone who heard him was amazed how well this young boy understood the laws and prophecies of the ancient books. Mary was angry at Jesus. "Son, why have you treated us like this?" she asked him. "Your father and I have been searching for you in great fear!"

"Why were you searching for me?" asked Jesus. "Didn't you know you could find me in my Father's house?" He was talking about the Temple, the House of God.

They returned to Nazareth. The Gospel of Luke says that from that day Jesus was obedient to his parents, grew in wisdom and was respected by his family and friends.

"His mother treasured all these things in her heart," says Luke.

The English artist William Holman Hunt traveled to Jerusalem to study Jewish customs and costume, and used local people as models for his painting *The Finding of the Savior in the Temple.*

CHRIST AMONG THE DOCTORS *by Paolo Veronese, 1560*

Compare Holman Hunt's painting with this work by Paolo Veronese, one of the greatest
artists of the Italian Renaissance.

Renaissance is a French word meaning *rebirth*. In the 15th and 16th centuries Europeans rediscovered
classical art, history, and philosophy. *Classical* means *coming from ancient Greece and Rome.*
The Renaissance was the rebirth of the classical styles and themes in art.

The Jerusalem Temple in Veronese's painting looks like a classical Greek or Roman temple with
marble columns and reliefs. The *doctors*, or teachers of faith, gathered at the Temple,
wear clothes of 16th century Venice where Veronese lived, rather than those of ancient Israel in the
days of Jesus. Renaissance artists told their stories using dramatic poses and grand gestures. There is
a lot of drama, tension, and movement in Veronese's painting. In comparison, William Holman Hunt
paints a much quieter scene. Jesus looks like a kid who had been lost and is happy to be with his
family again. He holds his mom's hand, and she hugs him. The gestures of Holman Hunt's characters
are simple, warm and real. You get a glimpse of ancient Jerusalem, with the blind beggar on the steps
of the Temple and the city stretching to the horizon below the Temple Mount.

THE SHADOW OF DEATH *by William Holman Hunt, 1870*

Here is another work seeking to create a glimpse into the life of Jesus in his family.
We see Jesus in a carpenter's workshop. He stretches his arms after a hard day of work.
Suddenly his mother notices a scary shadow on the tool rack on the wall. The shadow looks like
a man nailed to the cross. Crucifixion was the way the Romans put criminals to death. Since Judea
was under the rule of the Roman Empire, everyone knew how cruel was a death on the cross.
It looks like Mary was opening a wooden box with some treasures inside, when she saw the shadow
and froze in shock. The treasures inside the box are the gifts Jesus received from the Magi
as a baby. They remind us of the words Mary and the Magi heard from the angels, that Jesus would
grow up to be a King whose kingdom will have no end. There is a star in the stonework above the
window – a reminder of the Star of Bethlehem.

THE BAPTISM OF CHRIST
by Andrea del Verrocchio, 1472-1475

THE BAPTISM OF CHRIST

When Jesus had reached the age of about 30, he knew it was time to begin his *ministry.* *Ministry* is teaching and helping people. But first Jesus went to John the Baptist and was *baptized* in the Jordan River. John the Baptist went from village to village along the Jordan River, telling people to *repent*, that is to turn away from any wrongdoings, and to confirm their promise by dipping into the waters of Jordan in the ritual of *baptism*. Crowds of people followed John wondering if he was sent by God, if he was a savior the people of Israel were waiting for. "I am not the one you are waiting for," John told them. "I baptise you with water, but the one who is coming after me will baptize you with the Holy Spirit." He was talking about Jesus. So when Jesus came to John asking to be baptized, John said: "Why are you coming to me to be baptized? You should baptize me!" As Jesus was baptized in the river, he prayed. Suddenly, the Holy Spirit appeared over him in the form of a dove, and a voice came from heaven, saying: "You are my Son, whom I love." Churches celebrate the Feast of the Baptism of Jesus on January 6 (January 19, Julian calendar).

Andrea del Verrocchio was the teacher of Leonardo da Vinci. Remember Leonardo's *The Annunciation*? Art experts say they can see the hand of both Leonardo and Andrea in both *The Annunciation* and *The Baptism of Christ*. They say that in *The Baptism* the angel on the left and the landscape behind Jesus were painted by Leonardo in oil paint, while the rest of the work was done in tempera. Tempera is a type of paint made from color pigments mixed with egg yolk. It was widely used in the Middle Ages. Giorgio Vasari, a 16th-century historian of Art, says in his book *Lives of the Most Excellent Painters, Sculptors, and Architects*, that when Verrocchio saw the angel painted by Leonardo in *The Baptism of Christ* he decided that he was nowhere as good as his student, and quit painting!

THE APPEARANCE OF CHRIST BEFORE THE PEOPLE *by Alexander Ivanov, 1837–57*

It took Russian artist Alexander Ivanov 20 years to complete this painting. Ivanov was a master of creating characters that look very real. As Jesus comes toward the people who have just been baptized in the Jordan, not everyone believes John the Baptist that Jesus is the Son of God. Quite a few faces in the crowd look like they are saying, "Ha-ha, oh really?"

John wears clothing made of camel's hair, with a leather belt around his waist, as described in the Gospel of Mark. The colors of Jesus' clothes are red and blue – the colors of royalty, holiness, and sacrifice. To the left of John the Baptist are future *apostles,* disciples of Jesus – including John, Peter and Andrew. John is the youngest, he looks toward Jesus with hope.

The word *apostle* comes from the Greek word *apostolos* – *a messenger.*

The apostles took the message of Jesus' teaching and traveled, bringing it to people in many lands.

The word *disciple* comes from the Latin word *discipulus* – *a student.*

The style of Alexander Ivanov's work was typical of 19th century artists. It's called the *Academic* style, named after the *Academy of Fine Arts* in Paris. They also call it the *neo-classical* style. *Neo* means 'new.' It's a style that followed the principles of Renaissance art, including its strong interest in the themes of classical Greek and Roman culture. Like the art of the Renaissance, Academic, or neo-classical paintings have a lot of dramatic poses and gestures, and long, flowing, draped fabrics in solid colors. The bodies of people look strong and beautiful, like ancient Greek sculptures.

CHRIST IN THE DESERT *by Ivan Kramskoi, 1872*

THE TEMPTATION OF CHRIST

After being baptized by John the Baptist, Jesus spent 40 days and nights in the desert praying and thinking. He ate nothing during those days, and was hungry. While in the desert, the Devil appeared before Jesus and said to him, "If you are the Son of God, tell this stone to become bread."

Jesus answered, "Man shall not live on bread alone." So true! Strength is in faith, not in cheap magic.

The Devil wasn't happy with Jesus' response, so he took him to Jerusalem and had him stand on the highest point of the great Temple. "If you are the Son of God," he said, "throw yourself down from here. Your father will order his angels to lift you up and carry you back to safety."

Jesus answered, "The holy books say: Don't test God." Makes sense: If you trust someone, you don't need to test them. If you have faith, you don't need proof of God's love.

The Devil didn't give up. Next he tried to tempt Jesus with power.

He led him up on a high mountain, and showed him in an instant all the kingdoms of the world.

The Devil said, "I will give you all the power and glory of these kingdoms if you bow to me."

Jesus answered, "The holy books say: Serve only the Lord your God, and no one else."

Finally the Devil left, and Jesus returned to Galilee where he lived, to start his ministry.

In this painting by the Russian artist Ivan Kramskoi Jesus looks exhausted by hunger and sleeplessness. Kramskoi doesn't try to make Jesus look strong and powerful. His style is not Academic. It's *realistic.*

THE CALLING OF THE APOSTLES PETER AND ANDREW
by Duccio Di Buoninsegna, 1308-1311

One day while walking by the Sea of Galilee, Jesus saw two fishermen. They were brothers, Simon Peter and Andrew. Jesus called out to them, "Come and follow me and be my disciples." And they followed him. A little farther on, Jesus passed two brothers, James and John. They were fishermen too. He also called them to be his disciples, and they joined him as well. The Gospel of Luke tells us that Jesus asked Peter and his partners to cast their nets and catch some fish. "Master, we've worked hard all night and haven't caught anything," answered Peter.

But then he agreed, and when they cast the nets, the catch of fish was so huge that one boat was not enough to hold it. The fishermen figured this must be a miracle. On the shore Peter fell on his knees in front of Jesus and said, "Go away from me, Lord; I am a sinner!" *Sin* as a wrongdoing.

Peter thought that his life was not holy enough to deserve the company of Jesus.

But Jesus responded: "Don't be afraid; from now on you will fish for people."

So the future apostles pulled their boats up on the shore, left everything, and followed Jesus.

Italian artist Duccio di Buoninsegna worked in between two eras of European history –
the Middle Ages and the Renaissance. His style was typical of the Middle Ages.

His painting looks flat. It has a gold background, and no landscape or horizon behind the figures
of the apostles. It has no *perspective*. *Perspective* is showing objects that are closer to us – bigger,
and objects that are farther away – smaller. It makes paintings look 3-dimensional. But the artists
of the Middle Ages rarely used perspective, and didn't try to make their works look true to life.

THE CALLING OF SAINT MATTHEW *by Caravaggio, 1600*

THE CALLING OF MATTHEW THE APOSTLE

One day Jesus met a man named Matthew. Matthew collected taxes for the Roman government. Tax collectors were not liked in Israel, because they made people overpay their taxes so they could keep a lot of money for themselves. Matthew joined Jesus and his disciples, and later invited them to his home for dinner. Some teachers of religious law and faith learned about this and asked Jesus' disciples, "Why does your teacher eat with tax collectors and sinners?"
Jesus heard their question, and answered: "It is not the healthy who need a doctor, but the sick."

In his painting *The Calling of Saint Matthew* Italian artist Caravaggio shows Matthew the tax collector sitting at a table with his friends. Jesus and Peter have entered the room, and Jesus is pointing at Matthew. A beam of light illuminates the faces of the men at the table. Matthew points at himself "Me?" Caravaggio worked in the style of *mannerism* that came at the end of Renaissance. Mannerist artists experiemented with light and contrast: Bright patches of light on the faces of Matthew and his friends, and deep shadows around them create tension and the feeling of something important about to happen. Caravaggio never did sketches. He worked fast, laying paint in broad stokes, and always used real people as models for his characters.

WEDDING AT CANA

The Gospel of John says that Jesus performed his first public miracle at a wedding in the town of Cana in Galilee.

In the middle of the wedding feast, they ran out of wine. Mary said quietly to Jesus,

"They have no more wine."

But Jesus replied,

"My hour has not yet come."

Then Mary told the servants at the feast:

"Do whatever my son tells you."

Nearby stood six huge water jars. Jesus said to the servants,

"Fill them with water."

So they filled them to the brim. Then he told them,

"Now take some water from these jars, and take it to the host of the feast"

They did so.

THE MARRIAGE AT CANA *by Maerten de Vos, 1596*

The host tasted the water. The water had been turned into wine! He did not realize where it had come from, so he called the bridegroom aside and said,

"We usually serve the best wine first, but you have saved the best till now!"

Renaissance-era Flemish artist Maerten de Vos lived in Antwerp, located in modern Belgium.
In his painting *Marriage at Cana* the wedding reception is set in a typical Renaissance palace,
with all the guests, except Jesus and Mary, wearing Renaissance fashions. The groom wears
a crown of laurel leaves. De Vos was clearly not sure how people dressed in the times of Jesus.
Three musicians in the gallery upstairs play lutes. The lute was a popular musical instrument in those
times. Look at the 6 water jars: They are real works of art in this painting! Have you noticed:
There are 3 crowns hanging over the head of the bride? That was a custom in de Vos's time:
The crowns were there as a blessing, and as a reminder that God protects marriage and family.

WEDDING AT CANA BY *by Carl Bloch, 1870*

In the *Wedding at Cana* painting by Danish artist Carl Bloch, servants bring a glass of wine to the host of the feast. He looks surprised, an empty wine jar in his hands. One of the servants is pointing at Jesus. Carl Bloch's style is Academic. The setting of the feast is a Roman palace with marble columns and floors. The scene looks dramatic because it is *backlit*. *Backlit* means that the source of light is in the back, behind the main figures in the *foreground*. The *foreground* in a painting means the objects or people that appear to be closest to us, while the *background* is anything that looks like it is behind the things in the foreground.

THE SERMON ON THE MOUNT

One day big crowds followed Jesus, eager to hear his teaching. Jesus climbed up a hill where everyone could see him and explained the truths that became the basis of Christian teaching.

Jesus started with eight blessings, also called the *beatitudes*, from the Latin word *beatus* – 'blessed.'

Blessed are the poor in spirit, for theirs is the kingdom of heaven.

Blessed are those who mourn, for they will be comforted.

Blessed are the meek, for they will inherit the earth.

Blessed are those who hunger and thirst for righteousness, for they will be filled.

Blessed are the merciful, for they will be shown mercy.

Blessed are the pure in heart, for they will see God.

Blessed are the peacemakers, for they will be called children of God.

Blessed are those who are persecuted because of righteousness, for theirs is the kingdom of heaven.

Jesus called people of faith *the salt of the earth* and *the light of the world*. In the ancient world salt was almost as expensive as gold. Then, as now, both salt and light are needed to survive.

Jesus also compared the ancient laws of the Jewish faith with the new truths of his teaching. The old laws allowed you to take revenge on anyone who has harmed you: *An eye for an eye, a tooth for a tooth... Love your neighbor and hate your enemy*. Instead, Jesus said, "Love your enemies and pray for those who seek to harm you." Instead of revenge, give your enemies a chance to understand their errors and change their ways.

Jesus said that any acts of kindness and charity should be from the heart. You shouldn't do good works to have people praise you. "When you give to the poor," he said, "do it in secret. Then God, your Father, who sees what is done in secret, will reward you." "Do not store up for yourselves treasures on earth," he advised. Any material treasure, such as money or beautiful things, can be stolen or destroyed. The only treasures that are forever are faith, love, kindness, compassion, and helping people in need.

In this painting by William Holman Hunt, Jesus, carrying a lantern, knocks on the door. The lantern is a symbol of faith, and the door is a person's heart.

THE LIGHT OF THE WORLD *by William Holman Hunt, 1849*

SERMON ON THE MOUNT *by Carl Bloch, 1877*

In this painting, Carl Bloch captured the many emotions people feel as they hear the teachings of Jesus. There is a look of inspiration and hope on some faces. Others seem to be deep in thought — perhaps thinking about their life, or comparing Jesus' teaching with what they heard from other teachers of faith.

Meanwhile a little boy is trying to catch a colorful butterfly that has landed on his mom's head! Unless you open your heart like a child, taught Jesus, you will never enter the Kingdom of Heaven.

JESUS AND THE SAMARITAN WOMAN *by Henryk Siemiradzki, 1890*

 JESUS AND THE SAMARITAN WOMAN

One day Jesus traveled across Samaria, an area of Ancient Israel that lay between Galilee and Judea. Samaritans, the people of Samaria, shared faith with the rest of Israel, but they didn't go to the great Temple in Jerusalem. Instead, they worshipped God in the ruins of their own ancient temple that had been destroyed in war, in 110 BC. Samaritans didn't like the Jews who worshipped in Jerusalem, and the Jewish people of Judea and Galilee disliked the Samaritans. So when Jesus asked a Samaritan woman by a well for some water, she was surprised.

"You are Jewish," she told Jesus, "and I am a Samaritan. How can you ask me for a drink?"

If you knew who I am, answered Jesus, you would ask me for the water of life.

"Those who drink the water I give, will never be thirsty again," he said. "It will become a fresh, bubbling spring of eternal life." The Samaritan woman was puzzled.

"I know that when the *Messiah*, the Savior of Israel, comes, he will explain everything to us," she said. Many people in Israel believed that one day a Savior would come to free them from the Romans.

"I am the Savior," said Jesus. The woman ran back to her village, telling everyone about him.

The 19th-century Polish artist Henryk Siemiradzki painted this scene with a lot of attention to detail. The wild flowers, the clay water jar, and the woman's clothes, hair style and jewelry look especially realistic, almost like a photograph.

HEALING THE CENTURION'S SERVANT

Traditionally, we divide history into two parts – before and after the birth of Jesus. In English, we use the letters **BC**, which stand for *Before Christ*, when we talk about events that happened before Jesus. And we use the letters *AD*, which stand for *Anno Domini – in the year of the Lord* in Latin – for the years after Jesus was born. In 63 BC the Roman general Pompey conquered Jerusalem. Israel became a province of the Roman Empire. At the time of Jesus' ministry it was called the Province of Judea and was governed by Roman Procurator Pontius Pilate. The Romans collected taxes from their provinces. Nobody liked them in Israel, and there were lots of Roman troops around to make sure everyone obeyed the Roman laws.

As Jesus went from town to town, people often asked him to cure their sickness. Jesus healed them. The stories of his miracles spread, and more and more people followed him wherever he went. One day a Roman officer came to Jesus asking him to heal his servant who was very sick. The officer was a *centurion*. The word *centurion* comes from the Latin word *centum – a hundred*. A centurion commanded a hundred men. Such English words as *cent* and *century* also come from the Latin *centum*.

Jesus wanted to help the Centurion's servant, "Shall I come and heal him?" he asked. The Centurion replied, "Lord, I do not deserve to have you come under my roof. But just say the word, and my servant will be healed." When Jesus heard this, he was amazed, and turning to the crowd around him, he said, "I tell you, I have not found such great faith even in the land of Israel." That same hour the Centurion's servant was healed.

18th-century French artist Joseph-Marie Vien painted the Centurion on his knees, with his hands open, a gesture showing sincerity. Jesus points at the Centurion as he praises his faith.

THE CENTURION
KNEELING
AT THE FEET
OF CHRIST
by
Joseph-Marie Vien
1752

THE STORM ON THE SEA OF GALILEE *by Rembrandt, 1632*

One evening Jesus and his disciples were crossing the Sea of Galilee in a boat.

Jesus was sleeping. Suddenly, a storm came up. Waves swept over the boat.

The disciples of Jesus woke him, saying, "Lord, save us! We're going to drown!"

He replied, "You have so little faith! Why are you so afraid?"

Then he got up and told the wind to stop blowing, and said to the sea: "Peace! Be still!"

And the sea calmed down.

The disciples were amazed and kept asking each other:

"What kind of man is this? Even the winds and the waves obey him!"

Rembrandt is one of the greatest painters in the history of art. He was Dutch. During his time, in the 17th century, the Dutch Republic was so far ahead of most countries in Europe in trade, science and culture, that they call that era the ***Dutch Golden Age***.

The Storm on the Sea of Galilee is one of Rembrandt's most dramatic paintings, and it's his only ***seascape***. A ***landscape*** is a picture of the land, rivers, mountains, fields; a ***seascape*** is a picture of the sea or seashore. In this painting we see a small boat with a torn sail caught in a violent storm. Dark clouds are low, high waves with white foaming crests are pushing the boat toward the rocks. The apostles are working to hold the boat together. They are scared. One of the disciples is looking straight at us, as if hoping for help. Art experts think that this is Rembrandt's ***self-portrait***. When artists create their own portraits, they are called self-portraits.

Works by great masters of art are famous and sell for enormous amounts of money. Because of their huge value, some dishonest art dealers pay burglars to rob museums and steal precious paintings. In 1990 two thieves dressed as police officers broke into a museum in Boston and stole ***The Storm on the Sea of Galilee*** along with 12 other works. It was the biggest art theft in U.S. history. So far this crime remians unsolved. The museum displays the paintings' empty frames, and investigators from the FBI Art Crime Team are looking for the missing masterpieces.

The frame which once held Rembrandt's **The Storm on the Sea of Galilee** *at the* **Isabella Stewart Gardner Museum** *in Boston*

THE DAUGHTER OF JAIRUS *by Ilya Repin, 1871*

JESUS RAISES THE DAUGHTER OF JAIRUS FROM THE DEAD

News of the miracles of Jesus spread all over Israel. Jesus went through all the towns
and villages, teaching people about the Kingdom of Heaven and healing every disease and sickness.
When Jesus was teaching in Galilee a man named Jairus, who was a synagogue leader, came and fell
at Jesus' feet, asking him to come to his house: His only daughter, a girl of about twelve, was dying.
Jesus went to the house of Jairus. But the crowds of people who followed him were huge, and
everyone was begging him for help and healing. By the time Jesus reached the house of Jairus,
Jairus had received the sad news that his daughter had died.
Hearing this, Jesus said to Jairus, "Don't be afraid; just believe and she will be healed."
When they arrived at the house, Jesus did not let anyone go in with him except Peter, John, James,
and the child's father and mother. Meanwhile, the rest of the family stood crying outside.
"Stop crying," Jesus said. "She is not dead. She is just asleep."
 They refused to believe him, knowing that she was dead. But Jesus took the girl by the hand and
said, "My child, get up!" And at once she stood up, alive. Her parents were astonished and
so happy, but Jesus asked them not to tell anyone what had happened.

JESUS HEALS THE BLIND

The Gospels tell us that Jesus had a lot of
compassion for people he met on his way.
Many looked hopeless and helpless,
like sheep without a shepherd.
At some point a couple of blind men followed
Jesus asking him to heal them. Jesus asked:
"Do you believe that I am able to do this?"
"Yes, Lord," they replied.
Then he touched their eyes and said,
"According to your faith let it be done to you."
And all of a sudden, they could see again!
Jesus warned them,
"See that no one knows about this."
But they were so happy, they went out and
spread the news about him all over the country.

The two paintings on these pages –
The Daughter of Jairus and *Jesus Healing
the Blind Man* are by two Russian artists
who belonged to the Realist movement in
arts that grew throughout the 19th century.
Realists tried to represent life truthfully.
To them, all those dramatic poses, gestures,
Greek columns and Roman dresses

JESUS HEALING THE BLIND MAN
by Vasily Surikov, 1888

in Renaissance and Academic art looked unnatural and boring. They tried to make everything in
their paintings seem real, including the true feelings of their characters. Notice the expression on the
face of the blind man who is reaching for the ray of light, his walking stick falling from his hands.
You can almost see his hands and lips shaking, tears streaming from his eyes...
Notice how the poses of Jairus and his wife tell the story of hopelessness and grief at the loss of
their daughter. In both paintings the artists use light to draw our attention to the most important
things – the faces of Jesus and the dead girl... the flowers on her pillow... the hands
of the blind man...the eyes of Jesus...

THE MIRACLE OF THE LOAVES AND THE FISHES *by Joachim Patinir, 1520*

JESUS FEEDS 5000 PEOPLE

Jesus went to a remote area to be alone, but crowds of people followed him. He stopped and healed the sick. It was getting late in the day, and people were exhausted and hungry. Jesus wanted to offer them food, but his disciples had brought only five loaves of bread and two fish. Jesus prayed. He broke the loaves of bread and gave them to the disciples, who passed them to the people. The numbers of loaves and fish kept growing until more than 5000 people ate as much as they wanted.

Joachim Patinir was a Flemish artist from the city of Antwerp in present-day Belgium. He was one of the first artists to create landscapes as independent works of art. Painting the scene of this miracle of Jesus, Patinir fills most of his canvas with a beautiful detailed landscape. The colors of the trees and fields are yellow-green closest to us, and blue-green in the distance. This, and the skillful use of perspective, makes this landscape unusually realistic for 16th-century art.

JESUS WALKING ON WATER

After Jesus fed the crowds of hungry
people, he told his disciples to take a boat back
to the other side of the Sea of Galilee.
He stayed behind to pray alone.
Night fell, and a storm was rocking and
tossing the boat when, suddenly, the apostles
saw Jesus walking toward them on the water!
They were terrified.
"It's a ghost!" They cried out in fear.
But Jesus said, "Don't be afraid, it's me!"
"Lord, if it's you," Peter replied, "tell me
to come to you on the water."
"Come," said Jesus.
Peter got out of the boat, stepped onto the
water and started walking... He walked almost
all the way to Jesus. But then the wind
grew stronger and the waves rose high:
Peter became afraid and started to sink.

JESUS WALKS ON THE WATER
by Ivan Aivazovsky, 1890

"Lord, save me!" he called out to Jesus. Jesus reached out his hand and caught him.
"Why didn't you believe you could do this?" he asked Peter.
They climbed into the boat, and the wind died down.
Then the disciples bowed to Jesus, saying, "Truly you are the Son of God."

A famous Russian artist of the 19th century, Ivan Aivazovsky, was a master of seascapes.
He created a few *Jesus Walks on Water* paintings. They show Jesus glowing with miraculous
light, while the sea, the boat, and the disciples are painted very realistically. Notice how
the waves reflect the light that comes from Jesus.

To explain his teaching Jesus often told *parables*. *Parables* are easy-to-remember short stories with a lesson in each one. One of the most famous parables of Jesus is *The Parable of the Prodigal Son*. *Prodigal* is an old word that describes a person who wastes money.

"There was a man who had two sons," said Jesus. The younger son asked his dad to give him his inheritance now, because he wanted to travel and try his luck in business in faraway lands. But the young man was not smart in spending his dad's money: He wasted everything his dad gave him, and ended up poor and homeless. He found a job at a pig farm, but he was paid so little that the pigs were eating much better food than him. Finally, he went back to his dad. He thought his dad would be angry. Instead, his father ran to his son, threw his arms around him and kissed him. "Father, I have sinned against heaven and against you," said the young man. "I don't deserve to be called your son." But his father told his sevants: "Quick! Bring the best clothes for my son. Put a ring on his finger and sandals on his feet!... Let's have a feast and celebrate. For this son of mine was lost and is found." So they began to celebrate. Meanwhile the young man's brother was upset. He had worked all this time for his dad, and there had never been a celebration like this for him. "My son," the father said to him, "you are always with me, and everything I have is yours. But we had to celebrate and be glad, because we thought your brother was dead, but he is alive. He was lost and now is found." The father in this parable represents God's love, endlessly generous, without limits. There is no shame in admitting your mistakes and asking for forgiveness. God's mercy is for everyone who asks for it with sincerity and a pure heart. So Jesus taught.

The Return of the Prodigal Son was painted by Rembrandt shortly before he died. Some art experts call it *the greatest picture ever painted* because of how precisely and effortlessly Rembrandt expressed the powerful message of this parable. The loving gesture of the father's hands, the tilt of his head, the way his eyes are gazing down and into the distance, as if remembering something – all express forgiveness without any conditions. The kneeling, bent pose of the Prodigal Son makes you think he is crying. His clothes and shoes are worn away. With his hands locked together, the older son stands on the right. His face is sad, his lips are tight. He looks angry. The brothers' mom and their dad's advisor look on, surprised, from the dark. Rembrandt was so moved by this parable, he had been making dozens of drawings preparing to create it. He used the lighting to draw our attention to the most important things in his painting – the kneeling figure of the Prodigal Son, the face and hands of his dad, and the face and hands of the older brother.

The ancient books of Jewish Law commanded, "Love the Lord your God with all your heart, and love your neighbor as yourself." So one day a teacher of the Jewish faith asked Jesus, "And who is my neighbor?" Most people believed *neighbors* were people who lived in the same country and shared faith. But even though Jesus lived in Israel, he said he came to teach and save the whole world, not just the Israeli people. For him, a neighbor was any person of good will anywhere in the world. To explain this, he told the *Parable of the Good Samaritan.*

"A man was going down from Jerusalem to Jericho, when he was attacked by robbers," said Jesus. They stole his clothes, beat him up and went away, leaving him half dead. A priest who happened to be going down the same road saw the man, but crossed to the other side to avoid him.

Then came *a Levite* – a Temple guard. He too saw the wounded man, and he too ignored him.

Then came a Samaritan. As you remember, Samaritans didn't like the people of Judea, and certainly didn't think of them as *neighbors* they should help.

But when the Samaritan saw the wounded man, he stopped, washed his wounds, put him on his own donkey, brought him to an inn and gave money to the innkeeper to take care of him.

"Which of these three do you think was a neighbor to the man who was robbed?" asked Jesus.

"The one who helped him," said the teacher of the Law. Jesus told him, "So you should be like that Samaritan."

THE GOOD SAMARITAN
by Jacopo Bassano, 1563

Here are two paintings telling the story of the Good Samaritan. Jacopo Bassano was a student of Veronese, a famous Italian Renaissance painter from Venice. In keeping with Renaissance style, the poses of Bassano's characters are dynamic and dramatic. He uses rich intense red color to focus on the Good Samaritan's effort to lift the wounded man onto his donkey. Bassano also was famous for realistic paintings of animals and landscapes, and we see both in this work.

Maximilien Luce was a French artist who worked in the style called *Pointillism*. The word *Pointillism* comes from *point* – a dot, a spot. Pointillists painted in small dots. Each dot has a distinct color, but as we look at Pointillist paintings, our eyes mix the colors, and we see beautiful transitions and soft shapes. Pointillism became popular at the end of the 19th century. It grew out of a larger art movement, called *Impressionism*. Unlike Academic-style artists, Impressionists and Pointillists didn't blend and hide their brush strokes to make their paintings realistic. Instead, they wanted each brush stroke to be distinct and convey either movement or light.

THE GOOD SAMARITAN *by Maximilien Luce, 1896*

JESUS AT THE HOME OF MARTHA AND MARY *by Jacopo Tintoretto, 1580s*

JESUS AT THE HOME OF MARTHA AND MARY

A woman named Martha invited Jesus and his disciples to visit her home. She had a sister called Mary. Mary sat at Jesus' feet, listening to him while Martha was cooking and cleaning. Martha was upset that Mary was not helping her. She asked Jesus,
"Lord, don't you care that my sister has left me to do all the work by myself? Tell her to help me!"
"Martha," said Jesus, "you are worried about all these things, but there is only one thing that matters. Mary has chosen what is better. We should not take that away from her."
To Jesus, *the only thing that matters* is learning about faith. He wanted Martha to stop worrying about making a perfect party, and focus on the spiritual truths he brought to her family.

Tintoretto was from Venice, and belonged to the *Venetian School* of Italian Renaissance art, along with such amazing artists as Paolo Veronese, Jacopo Bassano, and Giovanni Bellini. He painted so fast, in such bold and large brush strokes, that they gave him the nickname *Furioso – furious*, in Italian. His style has many Mannerist features, such as high contrast, sudden splashes of light, and bold, often slanting, perspective. Compare Tintoretto's painting with that of Henryk Siemiradski. Tintoretto's Martha and Mary wear 16th-century dresses and jewelry, but in Siemiradzki's painting they look more like people who lived in Ancient Israel.

JESUS AT THE HOME OF MARTHA AND MARY *by Henryk Siemiradzki, 1886*

THE RAISING OF LAZARUS *by Rembrandt, 1630-1632*

The Raising of Lazarus

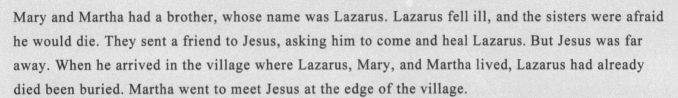

Mary and Martha had a brother, whose name was Lazarus. Lazarus fell ill, and the sisters were afraid he would die. They sent a friend to Jesus, asking him to come and heal Lazarus. But Jesus was far away. When he arrived in the village where Lazarus, Mary, and Martha lived, Lazarus had already died been buried. Martha went to meet Jesus at the edge of the village.

"Lord, if you had been here, my brother would not have died," she told him. "But I know that even now God will give you whatever you ask."

Soon Mary came out, and she, too, said to Jesus: "Lord, if you had been here, my brother would not have died."

Jesus was deeply moved by the sisters' grief. He cried, and asked them to show him the tomb of Lazarus. It was a cave with a stone laid across the entrance. "Take away the stone," Jesus said. When they took away the stone, Jesus called in a loud voice, "Lazarus, come out!"

And the dead man came out, his hands and feet wrapped with strips of cloth.

Rembrandt's painting *The Raising of Lazarus* shows the moment when Lazarus woke up from the sleep of death. Martha, Mary, and others are watching in amazement.

The *composition* of Rembrandt's painting is very simple. *Composition* is how different elements are placed in a painting.

There are three brightly-lit spots — Jesus' raised arm and face, the face of one of the sisters, and the face of Lazarus. Rembrandt creates a sense of surprise by surrounding Lazarus with dark empty space while everybody else is crowded on the opposite side of the painting. Created 100 years before Rembrandt's work, the *Raising of Lazarus* by Sebastiano del Piombo has all the features of the Renaissance style.

The artist creates the sense of excitement by filling every corner of his painting with moving bodies and dramatic gestures. Figures and light are distributed evenly over the painting, and the background is a beautiful landscape.

THE RAISING OF LAZARUS
by Sebastiano del Piombo, 1517–1519

The word *transfiguration* means a change in how a person looks, a change into a more beautiful or spiritual state. The Transfiguration is one of the miracles of Jesus. The Feast of The Transfiguration is celebrated on August 6 (August 19, Julian Calendar).

Jesus took with him the apostles Peter, James and John, and led them up a high mountain. There, he suddenly changed: His face shone like the sun, and his clothes became as white as a flash of lightning. Two prophets of Ancient Israel, Moses and Elijah, who lived many hundreds of years before Jesus, appeared before Jesus and talked with him. Suddenly a bright cloud covered the top of the mountain and the apostles heard the voice of God: "This is my Son, whom I love. Listen to him!"

When the disciples heard this, they fell face down on the ground, terrified.

But soon Jesus came and touched them. "Get up," he said. "Don't be afraid."

When they looked up, they saw no one except Jesus.

When they returned from the mountain, a man came up to Jesus and fell on his knees.

"Lord, have mercy on my son," he said. He explained that an evil spirit got hold of the boy, and every time his son tried to speak, he fell on the ground in pain. He couldn't talk.

"I asked your disciples to drive out the spirit, but they couldn't," said the man.

So they brought the boy to Jesus. When the evil spirit saw Jesus, it immediately threw the boy on the ground. The boy rolled around, grinding his teeth. He couldn't speak.

"If you can do anything, take pity on us and help us," begged the boy's dad.

"Everything is possible for one who believes," answered Jesus. Then he addressed the evil spirit: "You deaf and mute spirit, I command you, come out and leave the boy alone." And the spirit left. The boy was healed! Then the disciples came to Jesus and asked, "Why couldn't we heal him?"

"Because you have so little faith," replied Jesus. "Truly I tell you, if you have faith as small as a seed, you can say to this mountain, *Move from here to there*, and it will move. Nothing will be impossible for you."

One of the greatest masters of Renaissance art, Raphael, combined in one painting the Transfiguration miracle and the miracle of healing the boy. Jesus rises in the air with Elijah on the left and Moses on the right. The colors of the clothes worn by the three apostles on the mountain are symbolic: James: Green – *Hope*, Peter: Blue and gold – *Faith*, John: Red – *Love*.

There is a lot of movement: The boy's family members are pointing at him, and the disciples who have failed to heal him, point at Jesus. This was Raphael's last painting. He worked on it until his death in 1520. For him, healing meant more than recovery from illness. It was also the idea of God healing the world from evil. Also, the artist's name, *Raphael*, comes from the Bible. In Hebrew, the language of the Bible and of Ancient Israel, *Raphael* means *God Has Healed*.

THE TRANSFIGURATION *by Raphael, 1520*

Right after the miracle of the Transfiguration, Jesus mentioned to his disciples that he wouldn't be with them for much longer. He would be killed and rise from the dead on the third day.

The apostles wondered what his words meant, but Jesus knew that his ministry was drawing to an end.

Soon Jesus and his disciples headed to Jerusalem for the Jewish feast of Passover.

On the Mount of Olives overlooking Jerusalem Jesus stopped and cried. He knew that one day the great city of Jerusalem and its Temple would be destroyed.

"Your enemies will not leave one stone on another, " said Jesus looking at Jerusalem, "because you did not recognize the time of God's coming to you."

The 19th-century Spanish artist Enrique Simonet captured that moment in his painting *Flevit Super Illam – Cried Over It*, in Latin.

Jesus entered Jerusalem riding a donkey. Having heard of Jesus, many people came to meet him.

They laid their cloaks and green tree branches on the street in front of him, singing, "Blessed is he who comes in the name of the Lord." This scene is shown in *The Entry into Jerusalem* by Fra Angelico, an Italian artist of the late Middle Ages and Early Renaissance.

The style of Fra Angeico combines features of both Medieval art and the art of the Renaissance.

FLEVIT SUPER ILLAM *by Enrique Simonet, 1892*

There is hardly any perspective in his *The Entry into Jerusalem*. All the trees are the same size; there is no space between the figures of people. On the other hand, the faces of his characters look realistic. Fra Angelico was from Tuscany in Italy. His real name was Giovanni. *Fra Angelico* means *angelic friar* in Italian. Friars were monks who didn't live in a monastery, but traveled around, teaching and doing other work for the church. Fra Angelico was known for his kind and charitable character and humbleness. When he became famous as a painter he was invited to the Vatican, the center of the Catholic Church. The Pope offered to make him the archbishop of Florence, a position that would have given him authority and welath. But Fra Angelico refused. In 1982 the Catholic Church proclaimed Fra Angelico a saint and the patron of artists. The words written on his grave say:

The deeds that count on Earth are not the ones that count in Heaven...

in the name of Christ, I gave all I had to the poor. I, Giovanni, am the flower of Tuscany.

THE ENTRY INTO JERUSALEM *by Fra Angelico*

CHRIST DRIVING THE MONEY-LENDERS OUT OF THE TEMPLE *by Cecco del Caravaggio, 1610*

CLEANSING THE TEMPLE

In Jerusalem, Jesus visited the court of the Great Temple, and saw that it was filled with merchants
selling pigeons and goats for sacrifices at the Temple. There were also money changers, exchaging
Greek and Roman coins for Jewish shekels. The Gospel of John says that "making a whip of cords,
Jesus drove them all out of the Temple. And he poured out the coins of the money-changers, and
overturned their tables. And he told those who sold the pigeons,
'Take these things away; do not make my Father's house a house of trade.'"
Cecco del Caravaggio is a name given to an unknown Italian artist who was a student of Caravaggio,
and painted in the Mannerist style. As a kid he worked as Caravaggio's servant and as a model for
his paintings. These are the only things we know about Cecco. Like Caravaggio, Cecco uses strong
contrast between light and dark. In this painting we see the same broad beam of light streaming down
from a window high above, as in Caravaggio's *The Calling of Saint Matthew.* The poses of Cecco's
characters are very dramatic, and everyone except Jesus is dressed in 17th century clothes.

JUDAS ISCARIOT

Meanwhile, priests from the great Jerusalem Temple and some teachers of faith decided that Jesus was dangerous. His teaching was all about about the Kingdom of Heaven. What if his followers stopped paying the Temple Tax, stopped sending money to pay the priests, or stopped bringing gifts and sacrifices to the Temple? The enemies of Jesus gathered at the palace of the High Priest, whose name was Caiaphas. They came up with a plan to arrest Jesus secretly and kill him. Then one of the twelve disciples of Jesus, whose name was Judas Iscariot, went to the chief priests and asked, "How much will you pay me if I betray Jesus to you?" So they counted out for him thirty silver coins. From then on Judas watched for an opportunity to hand Jesus over to them.

Here is a *fresco* from The Collegiata Santa Maria Assunta church in Italy, painted by Lippo Memmi around 1340. A *fresco* is a painting done in *watercolor* on wet *plaster* – a white material they used to cover walls and ceilings.
In the Middle Ages in Europe, most people were illiterate. They couldn't read or write. The church services were in Latin. Latin had stopped being an everyday spoken language since the fall of the Roman Empire. Common people didn't understand it. So churches hired artists to paint frescoes that told Bible stories and explained the main ideas of Christian faith on the church walls.

Here, on the left you see the fresco showing Judas accepting money from the chief priests. On the right you see how this story fits into a whole series of paintings about the last week of Jesus life – Entry into Jerusalem, Judas' betrayal, and the Last Supper.

JUDAS *by Lippo Memmi, 1340*

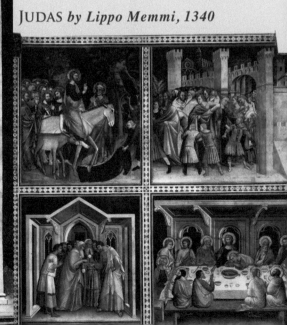

JESUS WASHING PETER'S FEET *by Ford Madox Brown, 1852*

JESUS WASHES THE FEET OF THE APOSTLES

Since most people in Ancient Israel either walked barefoot or wore sandals, it was a custom to offer guests water to wash their feet. Sometimes the host would wash his guests' feet as a sign of respect. So when Jesus and his disciples gathered to celebrate the Feast of the Passover, Jesus washed the apostles' feet, drying them with a towel he had wrapped around his waist.

English artist Ford Madox Brown paints this scene with the bright colors and realism of the Pre-Raphaelite style. Peter holds his hands in prayer. Peter's face is the portrait of William Hollman Hunt whose paintings you have seen in this book. A purse with 30 silver coins lies on the table. The disciples are sad. They realize that Jesus would not be the King in the land of Israel, after all. His Kingdom is "not of this world," and very soon he would leave them.

THE LAST SUPPER

The Last Supper was actually the traditional Passover celebration meal Jesus shared with his disciples. At the table, Jesus took bread, broke it and gave it to his disciples, saying, "Take it; this is my body given for you. Do this in remembrance of me." And he offered them a cup of wine, saying "This is my blood of the *covenant*, which is poured out for many." A *covenant* is an agreement. Jesus pointed out that his sacrifice would create an agreement between all the people of the world and God.
Jesus also said "Truly I tell you, one of you will betray me." One by one the disciples started saying, "Surely you don't mean me?" And Peter said, "Lord, I am ready to go with you to prison and to death." But Jesus answered him, saying, "I tell you, Peter, before the rooster crows today, you will deny three times that you even know me."

Joan de Joanes, a Spanish Renaissance artist, portrays Jesus holding a round wafer that represents bread, the body of Christ. On the table in front of him is the cup of wine. Jesus' left hand is on his heart, in a gesture of sincerity. He offers his sacrifice to anyone who would follow his teaching and his example. Meanwhile, Judas is hiding the purse with his 30 silver coins behind his back.

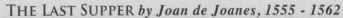

THE LAST SUPPER *by Joan de Joanes, 1555 - 1562*

Agony is deep, tragic suffering. After the Last Supper, Jesus and three of his disciples went to the Garden of Gethsemane to pray. The garden was at the foot of the Mount of Olives. As they walked into the garden, Jesus became sad and anxious, and he asked his disciples:

"My soul is filled with sorrow to the point of death. Stay awake with me."

Going a little farther, he fell with his face to the ground and prayed,

"My Father, if it is possible, may this cup be taken from me. Yet not as I will, but as you will."

The **cup** is an ancient symbol of **fate** – things that happen to you whether you like it or not.

For Jesus, the cup was a symbol of his suffering and death.

When Jesus came back to his disciples, he found them asleep.

"Couldn't you stay awake and pray with me for even one hour?" he asked Peter.

He went away a second time and prayed, "My Father, if it is not possible for this cup to be taken away unless I drink it, may your will be done."

He came back seeking support from his disciples, but they were still asleep.

So he prayed again, alone, and an angel from heaven appeared to him and strengthened him.

Then he returned to the disciples and said to them, "Are you still sleeping? Look, the hour has come. Rise! Let's go! Here comes my betrayer!"

Over the centuries, when painting the scene in the Garden of Gethsemane artists often showed an angel handing Jesus the gold cup, the symbol of his suffering. Sandro Boticelli, an Italian artist of the Early Renaissance, paints Jesus leaning toward the angel, his hands crossed on his chest, as if saying from the depth of his heart "Your will be done."

PRAYER IN THE GARDEN
by Sandro Boticelli, 1500

El Greco was a Greek artist who worked in Spain, at the end of the Renaissance era. He painted his *Agony in the Garden* 100 years after Boticelli's *Prayer in the Garden*. Again, we see Jesus in red, an angel with the golden cup, and the sleeping disciples. But El Greco's style is very different. Like Caravaggio's, his art is often descibed as *Mannerist*.

By the end of the Renaissance, many young artists were getting tired of the realistic and beauty-focused art of Raphael, Michelangelo, Leonardo da Vinci, Veronese and other Renaissance masters. In their paintings people looked realistic, their bodies sculpted with soft light and shade. The landscapes had perspective and depth. The composition – or structure – of their paintings was always clear and well-balanced. So young artists started looking for new ways to express ideas and emotions. They started playing with light and shade, distorting the proportions of the human body, sometimes throwing the composition of a painting out of balance in order to create a sense of tension, surprise, or mystery. That's how Mannerism was born. In El Greco's paintings the figures are always pale and stretched, their faces, arms, and fingers long. The sky, mountains, and trees look like they are in motion. And the light is white and blinding, like a flash of lightning.

AGONY IN THE GARDEN *by El Greco, 1605*

JUDAS' KISS

While Jesus was still in the Garden of Gethsemane, Judas arrived there with a large crowd armed with swords and clubs, sent by the chief priests. Judas had arranged a signal:

"The one I kiss is the man – arrest him," he said. So he kissed Jesus, and the guards seized him. Peter tried to defend Jesus. He drew his sword, and struck one of the armed men, cutting off his ear.

"Put your sword back in its place," Jesus told him, "All who draw the sword will die by the sword." Then all his disciples ran away and hid so they would not get arrested with Jesus.

This beautiful illustration, *The Judas' Kiss*, is from *a book of hours* created for the Queen of France, Anne of Brittany, and illustrated by her court artist Jean Bourdichon. *A book of hours* is a prayer book. By 1450 Johannes Gutenberg had built the first printing press, and printed books started appearing toward the end of the 15th century. However, until then, all books were *manuscripts* copied by hand, and *illuminated*, or illustrated, by artists. Illustrations couldn't be easily copied, so illustrated books were rare and precious.

Like most manuscript illuminators, Jean Bourdichon used a lot of gold paint. The halo over Jesus' head, the lanterns, and a splash of light on his hair and shoulder give a magical touch to this scene. The expression on Jesus' face is sad but peaceful, and his hand touches the ear of the wounded guard.

There is harmony and an even flow in how the light and the figures are distributed in this illustration.

THE JUDAS' KISS
by Jean Bourdichon, 1503-1508

Compare Jean Bourdichon's illustration with *The Taking of Christ* by Caravaggio.

In Caravaggio's painting the arrest of Jesus happens in complete darkness. There is an expression of suffering on Jesus' face. His hands are clasped together. Judas and a soldier in black armor grab him at the same time. The apostle John rushes away into the darkness screaming, as the soldiers snatch his cloak. The figures in the painting seem to be tilting and almost falling, all in the same direction. It's a scary scene. The man on the right who holds a lantern is Caravaggio's self-portrait. His face is calm as he is looking at John running away in panic. Maybe what Caravaggio was trying to say with this painting was: Many centuries after the death and resurrection of Jesus people understand him better than his own friends and disciples did during his lifetime.

Caravaggio's own life had a lot of dangerous turns. His father died when he was a kid. Caravaggio studied art in Milan, but at 21 he got into a fight, wounded a police officer, and escaped to Rome with no money or friends. In Rome he managed to start a career as an artist, and became famous, but he never learned to control his anger. Soon, he got into another street fight, accidentally killed a man, was sentenced to death and had to hide. His powerful friends got him out of trouble, but when he was 35 another fight resulted in another death. He fled to Naples, then Malta, then Sicily. He was in court and in jail many times, and died of fever at 38 on his way to receive a pardon in Rome.

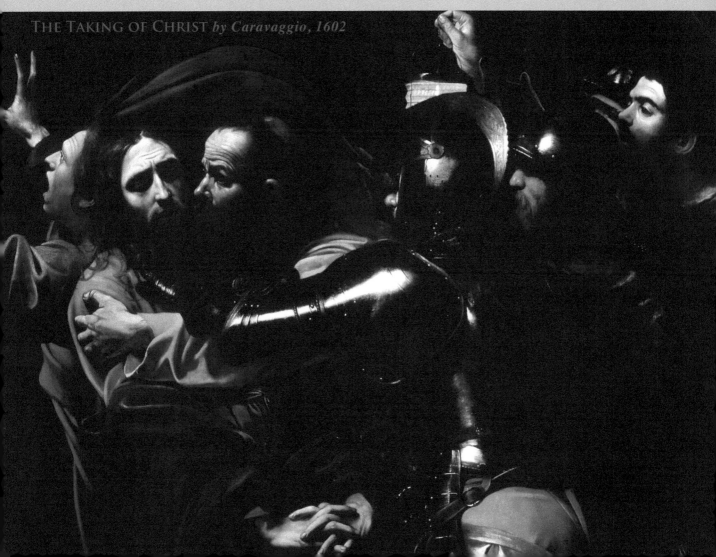

THE TAKING OF CHRIST *by Caravaggio, 1602*

THE DENIAL OF SAINT PETER *by Gerard Seghers, 1620*

THE DENIAL OF PETER

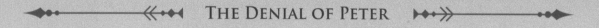

After the soldiers and the guards had seized Jesus, they took him to the High Priest's house. The apostle Peter followed at a distance and when the soldiers sat by the fire in the middle of the High Priest's courtyard, Peter sat down with them. A servant girl saw him and said, "This man was with him." But Peter denied it. "Woman, I don't know him," he said. The girl told the soldiers, "This man is one of them." But Peter denied it again. Finally, the people around the fire said to him, "Sure, you are one of them. Your Galilean accent gives you away." "I don't know that man!" cried out Peter. Immediately a rooster crowed. Then Peter remembered what Jesus had said: "Before the rooster crows, you will disown me three times." Peter went outside and cried bitterly.

The Denial of Saint Peter by Gerard Seghers was painted 10 years after the death of Caravaggio, but so strong was Caravaggio's influence on the painting style of the early 17th century, that dozens of artists all over Europe kept copying his style for many years. Gerard Seghers who lived in Antwerp was one of these *Caravaggist* artists. His works were realistic, with sharp transitions from light to darkness, and characters that looked like they had stepped into his paintings from the streets, markets and taverns of 17th-century Europe.

HE IS WORTHY OF DEATH *by Vasily Polenov, 1906*

JESUS BEFORE THE SANHEDRIN

The **Sanhedrin** was a court of 23 judges who were mostly chief priests. They gathered at the house of High Priest Caiaphas. The gospels say that the judges of the Sanhedrin were looking for false evidence against Jesus so that they could put him to death. They found a man who told them that Jesus had said he could destroy the Jerusalem Temple and rebuild it in three days.

The High Priest asked Jesus if that was true, but Jesus didn't answer. The High Priest got angry.

"Tell us the truth," he demanded, "are you the Messiah, the Son of God?"

"You have said so," Jesus replied.

Then the High Priest tore his own clothes, crying, "He has spoken blasphemy!"

Blasphemy means words disrespectful of God.

"What do you think?" Caiaphas asked the other members of the Sanhedrin.

"He is worthy of death," they answered.

Russian artist Vasily Polenov captured the moment when the High Priest tears his clothes in anger. Closer to the end of the 19th century more Europeans started traveling to the Middle East and the biblical lands. Historical paintings became more accurate. Polenov's father was an archaeologist who worked on archaeological digs in Greece and other ancient sites. In his paintings portraying the life of Jesus, Vasily Polenov tried to re-create the costume and customs of Ancient Israel.

Jesus before Pontius Pilate

Pontius Pilate was the Roman Procurator, or Governor, of Judea. When they brought Jesus before him, he asked: "Are you the king of the Jews?"

"My kingdom is not of this world," answered Jesus. "The reason I was born and came into the world is to testify to the truth. Everyone on the side of truth listens to me."

"What is truth?" asked Pilate. With this he went out to Jesus' accusers and said, "I don't think he has committed any crime. But it is your custom that we release one prisoner at the time of the Passover. Do you want me to release this 'king of the Jews'?"

But the enemies of Jesus wanted him to die. They had gathered a huge crowd outside chanting: "Crucify him! Crucify him!" They asked for another prisoner to be released, not Jesus.

Pilate didn't feel good sending Jesus to die. Instead he told his soldiers to beat him with whips. The soldiers mocked Jesus for being called 'the king.' They twisted together a crown of thorny branches and put it on his head. They also dressed him in red robes, put a stick in his hand like a scepter, slapped him on his face, and spit on him. Pilate thought that when the crowd outside saw Jesus mocked and beaten, they might feel sorry for him. So he brought him outside covered in blood and wearing a crown of thorns. "Look, here is the man," announced Pilate. These words are often quoted in Latin, *Ecce homo.* But the angry crowd still demanded that Jesus be crucified. Pilate was afraid that the situation was heading toward a major riot in Jerusalem, so he handed Jesus over to be crucified. Then he washed his hands in front of the crowd. "I am innocent of this man's blood," he said.

ECCE HOMO *by Antonio Ciseri, 1871*

Antonio Ciseri was a 19th century Swiss artist who created paintings for churches in Switzerland and Italy. He followed Renaissance and Academic art traditions. In his *Ecce Homo*, the scene is depicted from the point of view of the Romans, puzzled how some crazy Galilean who called himself *a king* could cause such hate in Jerusalem. Just like Ciseri, Russian artist Nikolai Ge also presents the conversation between Jesus and Pilate through the eyes of the Romans, maybe Pilate's guards. Pilate is tall and confident. He stands in bright sunlight. In the shade, by the wall, Jesus looks defeated. He doesn't look like a king at all. In contrast, Mihály Munkácsy, a Hungarian artist working around the same time as Ciseri and Ge, shows Jesus and Pilate through the eyes of the people in the courtyard of Pilate's palace. We see anger and chaos, as the crowd is yelling "Crucify him!" We also see people scared, ashamed, and shocked at the cruelty of Jesus' accusers.

WHAT IS TRUTH? *by Nikolai Ge, 1890*

ECCE HOMO *by Mihály Munkácsy, 1881*

THE CRUCIFIXION

Jesus carried his cross on the way to his crucifixion, but he was probably too exhausted, so the Roman guards grabbed a man they ran into, whose name was Simon, and they forced him to carry the cross part of the way. Soon they came to a place called *Golgotha*, the Skull Mountain. Jesus' hands and feet were nailed to the cross, and he was lifted up to die. Two robbers were being crucified at the same time. Crucifixion was an extremely cruel and barbaric punishment. A crucified person was left hanging on the cross until he died of pain, blood loss, and heart failure. Modern doctors think that a person's heart simply stopped after some hours on the cross.

Jesus' mother, his disciples, and a crowd of his accusers stood nearby. A Roman centurion with his soldiers guarded the crosses. The soldiers took Jesus' clothes and divided them between themselves, casting lots. A note nailed to Jesus cross said "The king of the Jews." People who passed by mocked Jesus, saying, "Come down from the cross, if you are the Son of God!"

Two paintings from the Renaissance era, by Raphael, and by the German artist, Lucas Cranach the Elder, capture the tragedy of the last hours of Jesus' life.

CHRIST CARRYING THE CROSS *by Raphael, 1516*
CHRIST CARRYING THE CROSS *by Lucas Cranach the Elder, 1503*

One of the crucified criminals said to Jesus: "Aren't you the Savior? Save yourself and us!"
But the other criminal stopped him. "We are punished justly," he said, But this man has done
nothing wrong." Then he called to Jesus: "Jesus, remember me when you come into your kingdom."
Jesus answered him, "Truly I tell you, today you will be with me in heaven."
The Gospel of Luke says that before Jesus died he said: "Father, into your hands I commit my spirit."
The moment he died a darkness came over the whole land and lasted for three hours.
A man called Joseph of Arimathea, a member of the Sanhedrin who didn't participate in
the chief priests' plot to kill Jesus, asked Pilate for Jesus' body. He took it down, wrapped it in a cloth
and placed it in a tomb cut in rock nearby.
In his **Dead Christ** painting, Italian Renaissance artist Giovanni Bellini created a timeless image
of grief, with Mary refusing to believe that Jesus was dead, and John looking away hopelessly, his face
frozen in despair.

DEAD CHRIST WITH MARY AND THE APOSTLE JOHN *by Giovanni Bellini, 1460*

The chief priests asked Pilate to have Roman soldiers guard the tomb of Jesus. They recalled that Jesus said *After three days I will rise again*. They didn't believe Jesus would rise from the dead, but they thought his disciples might steal his body and tell everyone 'Jesus has risen.' The moment of Jesus' resurrection is not described in the Gospels, but throughout the centuries many artists painted a scene where the rock tomb opens, the guards fall on the ground or run away, blinded by the light – and Jesus reappears alive.

THE RESURRECTION *by Paolo Veronese, 1570*

On the third day after Jesus
died, at dawn, some women
who were his followers,
went to his tomb.
The huge stone that
had been blocking
the door, was lying nearby,
an angel sitting on it.
There was a light like
lightning all around the angel,
and his clothes were white
as snow. The angel said
to the women,
"Do not be afraid, for I know
that you are looking for
Jesus, who was crucified.
He is not here; he has risen,
just as he said." The women
ran and told this news to
the apostles, but the apostles
didn't believe them. Peter,
however, got up and ran
to the tomb. Bending over,
he saw strips of cloth
in the tomb, including the
cloth that had covered the face
of Jesus, but Jesus' body
was gone. Peter left, wondering
what had happened.

WOMEN AT THE TOMB
by William-Adolphe Bouguereau
1876

The Gospel of John says that Mary Magdalene, one of Jesus' followers from Galilee, was crying by the empty tomb. She turned around to see a man standing behind her. She thought maybe he was a gardener, and maybe he had removed the body of Jesus.

"Sir, if you have carried him away, tell me where you have put him," she asked.

Suddenly the man said, "Mary," and she realized the man was Jesus!

"Teacher!" she cried and rushed to him, but Jesus stopped her.

"Do not hold on to me, for I have not yet gone to heaven, to the Father. Go instead to my brothers and tell them, *I am going to heaven, to my Father and your Father, to my God and your God.*"

Mary Magdalene went to the disciples with the news: "I have seen the Lord!"

Both paintings on these pages reflect the great wonder and mystery of Jesus' resurrection. The speechless amazement of the women at the tomb, and the surprise of Mary Magdalene, afraid to believe that Jesus is not dead, are shown through their poses, wide-open eyes, and the uncertain gestures of their hands. Both Willian-Adolphe Bouguereau and Alexander Ivanov were Academic painters, but there is a lot of realism in how they portray the emotions of these characters.

CHRIST'S APPEARANCE TO MARY MAGDALEN
by Alexander Ivanov, 1835

THE SUPPER AT EMMAUS *by Giuseppe Vermiglio*

Later on the same day, two of Jesus' disciples traveled to a village called Emmaus, not far from Jerusalem. On the road another traveler joined them, and they told him about the life and death of their teacher, Jesus of Nazareth. The traveler seemed to know a lot about the prophecies in the ancient books of Israel, which we now know as the Old Testament of the Bible. He explained to the two disciples, that Jesus was the Savior, or the *Messiah*, whom the people of Israel had been waiting for.

In Hebrew, the language of Ancient Israel, the *Messiah* means *the annointed one*. To *annoint* is to pour precious aromatic oil onto a person's head or hands. When a man became a king or a priest in Ancient Israel, they held the ritual of annointing to show that his authority came from God.

As the travelers reached Emmaus, the disciples invited their new friend to stay for supper with them at a local inn. At the table, the mysterious traveler broke a loaf of bread, said a prayer of thanks, and offered the bread to the apostles. Suddenly they realized he was Jesus himself! But just as they recognized him, he disappeared. The apostles both started talking at once, asking each other, "Were not our hearts burning within us while he talked with us on the road and opened to us the secrets of the ancient books?" Then they jumped up and ran back to Jerusalem.

There, as they were telling their story to the other Apostles, they suddenly heard the words: "Peace be with you" and looked up to see Jesus himself standing among them. They thought it was a ghost, but Jesus said, "Look at the wounds in my hands and my feet. It is I, myself!" They stood speechless around him in joy and amazement.

"Do you have anything here to eat?" asked Jesus. They gave him a piece of fish, and he ate.

"Here is what is written in the ancient books," Jesus said, "The Messiah will suffer and rise from the dead on the third day...You are witnessing these things happening."

Like many artists of the early 17th century, Giuseppe Vermiglio was influenced by Caravaggio. In his *Supper at Emmaus* you recognize many elements of Caravaggio's style: A hidden source of bright light, big realistic figures, a dark wall behind them, deep shadows. One of the disciples is looking at Jesus in a way that makes you think it is the very moment when he recognized Jesus.

DOUBTING THOMAS

Meanwhile, Thomas, one of the twelve apostles, was not with the disciples when Jesus appeared. He didn't believe their story of speaking with Jesus. "Unless I see the nail marks in his hands and touch his wounds, I will not believe," he said.

A week later the disciples were together again, and this time Thomas was with them. Though the doors were locked, Jesus appeared and stood among them again saying "Peace be with you!" Then he said to Thomas, "Put your finger here." He pointed at the wounds in his hands and the wound in his side, which had been pierced by a Roman soldier's spear.

Thomas touched the wounds and said to him, "My Lord and my God!"

Then Jesus told him, "Because you have seen me, you have believed. Blessed are those who have not seen and yet have believed."

This painting by Caravaggio is probably the most famous illustration of this story from the Gospel of John.

DOUBTING THOMAS *by Caravaggio, 1602*

The Acts of the Apostles, one of the books of the **New Testament** of the Bible, tells us that Jesus appeared to the apostles for 40 days after his resurrection. He taught them about the Kingdom of Heaven and instructed them to share the good news of his resurrection. On one occasion, while he was eating with them, he told them: "Do not leave Jerusalem, but wait for the gift my Father promised. For John the Baptist baptized people with water, but in a few days you will be baptized with the Holy Spirit." His disciples still didn't quite understand what the Kingdom of Heaven was. "Are you going to make Israel a powerful kingdom again?" they asked him. But Jesus responded by saying, "You will receive the power of the Holy Spirit, and you will share the truth about me here and to the ends of the Earth."

After he said this, he rose into Heaven before their very eyes, and a cloud hid him from their sight. **Ascension** means **rising**.

In the early 17th century, Renaissance features in art gradually disappeared, and Mannerism gave way to the **Baroque** style. The word **Baroque** comes from a Portuguese word **barroco** – a pearl of an irregular shape. The Baroque style used sharp contrast and dramatic movement to create a sense of grandness and awe. Baroque artists loved bright light, brilliant colors, and lots of decoration. Often the proportions of figures and objects in paintings were stretched, much like in El Greco's works. You see all these features in this painting by the Spanish Baroque artist Francisco Camilo.

THE ASCENSION
by Francisco Camilo, 1651

50 days after the resurrection of Jesus, on the Jewish feast of *Pentecost*, apostles and other followers of Jesus gathered together for the celebration. Suddenly a sound like the strong wind came from heaven. They saw what seemed to be tongues of fire come down and rest on each of them. All of them were filled with the Holy Spirit and began to speak in foreign languages they didn't know! People outside heard this and couldn't believe thair ears – a big crowd gathered around the house. Then Peter spoke to the crowd. "You put Jesus to death," he said to the people of Jerusalem, "But God raised him from the dead, freeing him from the agony of death, because it was impossible for death to keep its hold on him...God has sent the Holy Spirit – this is what you now see and hear." And about three thousand people in Jerusalem asked to be baptized and became Christians on that day. The story of the Pentecost is told in the *New Testament* book *The Acts of the Apostles.*

Pentecost by Jean Restout II showcases the best of the Baroque style. In his painting tongues of flame descend on the apostles and Mary in swirling clouds of smoke. With her hands on her heart, Mary is completely calm. She had never doubted that Jesus was the Son of God. In contrast, many of Jesus' disciples look shocked and even rush out of the building. After a lot of questioning and doubt, they still struggle to understand their experience of knowing Jesus.

PENTECOST *by Jean Restout II, 1732*

PORTRAITS OF THE ARTISTS

*Leonardo Da Vinci
self-portait*

*Alexander Ivanov
by Sergey Postnikov*

*Gerard David
self-portrait*

Rembrandt self-portrait

Raphael – self-portrait

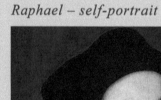

Carl Bloch

Vasily Surikov – self-portrait

Henryk Siemiradzki

Joseph Marie Vien
by Joseph Siffred Duplessis

John Everett Millais

Giovanni Bellini

Lucas Cranach the Elder

William Holman Hunt

Paolo Veronese – self-portrait

Joachim Patinir by Albrecht Dürer

Sandro Botticelli
self-portrait

Antonio Ciseri – self-portrait

Maximilien Luce

El Greco
self-portrait

Jacopo Bassano self-portrait

Tintoretto
self-portrait

Edward Burne-Jones

Ilya Repin – self-portrait

Vasily Polenov by Ilya Repin

Caravaggio by Ottavio Leoni

Léon Cogniet – self-portrait

Enrique Simonet – self-portrait

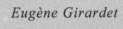

Fra Angelico
self-portrait

Eugène Girardet

Arthur Hughes – self-portrait

Jean Restout II – self-portrait

Gerard Seghers
by Anthony van Dyck

Ivan Kramskoi – self-portrait

Nikolai Ge – self-portrait

Ivan Aivazovsky – self-portrait

Ford Madox Brown
self-portrait

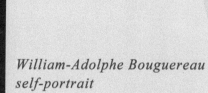

William-Adolphe Bouguereau
self-portrait

www.ingramcontent.com/pod-product-compliance
Lightning Source LLC
Chambersburg PA
CBHW040342201224
19273CB00002B/17